I don't want to!

Kitty always seems to be in trouble. She doesn't want to brush her teeth, or eat vegetables, or go to bed, or tidy her room – until something happens to make her change her mind, that is!

BEL MOONEY

I
don't
want
to!

Illustrated by Margaret Chamberlain

mammoth

For Alice, Maisie,
Kitty, Heather and Grace

First published in Great Britain 1985
by Methuen Children's Books Limited

This edition first published in 2001 by Mammoth
an imprint of Egmont Children's Books Limited
a division of Egmont Holding Limited
239 Kensington High Street, London W8 6SA
for The Book People Ltd
Hall Wood Avenue, Haydock, St Helens WA11 9UL

Text copyright © 1985 Bel Mooney
Illustrations copyright © 1985 Margaret Chamberlain

The moral rights of the author and illustrator have been asserted

ISBN 0 7497 0420 9

1 3 5 7 9 10 8 6 4 2

A CIP catalogue record for this title
is available from the British Library

Printed in Great Britain
by Cox & Wyman Ltd, Reading, Berkshire

Contents

I don't want to Clean my Teeth

Once there was a little girl called Kitty who didn't want to clean her teeth. Each night she would cry and scream and throw her toothbrush to the ground. One night she even wrote her name in toothpaste on the bathroom wall. "I *won't* clean my teeth," she said.

Kitty's mum was cross. "If you don't

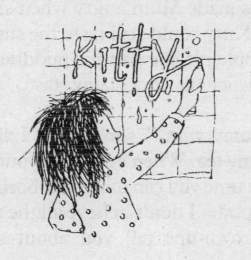

clean your teeth they will all fall out," she said.

"I don't care," said Kitty. "I want to have a mouth with no teeth in it, just like Grandad's."

"How will you be able to chew your food?" asked Mum.

"I will only eat soup and Instant Whip and porridge," said Kitty, "because they don't need any chewing!"

That night Kitty went to bed without cleaning her teeth. She put her finger in her mouth and tried to get out a piece of meat that was stuck in her tooth. It always made Mum angry when she did that. Kitty could still taste the sugar on the apple pie she had for pudding, and the delicious chocolatey taste of the cocoa.

"Yum, yum," she said. "I like to taste my tea. When you clean your teeth all the time you can only taste boring old toothpaste. I don't believe all the things the grown-ups tell you about sweets

making your teeth fall out – and anyway, I don't CARE!"

And Kitty took a sweet from the packet she had hidden under her pillow, and chewed it happily. Then she turned over and fell asleep.

Kitty started to dream. She dreamt that she was walking in a huge, dark wood, where the trees grew thickly and no birds sang. Suddenly she heard a loud cry. She ran towards the sound, and there in a clearing she saw little Red Riding Hood with the wolf. But it wasn't Little Red Riding Hood who was crying, it was the wolf!

Red Riding Hood kicked the wolf sharply on his knee and laughed. "I'm not afraid of you any more, because you're just a silly old toothless has-been," she shouted.

The wolf turned to Kitty and she saw

that it was true. He had no teeth.

"Where are your teeth?" Kitty asked.

"They all fell out," the wolf sighed. "I didn't ever clean them after I had eaten the children and animals, when I was the Big Bad Wolf. Now I can't be a Big Bad Wolf because who ever heard of a Big Bad Wolf without any teeth?" The wolf started to cry. "The other day," he sobbed, "I tried to frighten the Three Little Pigs, but they just laughed and said that when I blew their house down they'd give me some rice pudding for my gums."

Red Riding Hood poked him in the eye with her finger. "Yah, stupid old gummy!"

"Anybody whose job is being horrid has to have teeth," said the wolf sadly. "Otherwise people aren't afraid of him."

Kitty gasped. "But I want to be horrid," she said.

"Then you mustn't let your teeth fall out," said the wolf.

Red Riding Hood led him away, sticking twigs into his back, and laughing all the time.

Kitty woke up from the dream, and rushed into the bathroom. She was cleaning her teeth very carefully when Mum came in.

"There's my good little girl," smiled Mum, patting Kitty gently upon her head. "Now you'll have pretty white teeth when you're a big girl, won't you, darling?"

But Kitty looked into the bathroom mirror, and snarled. It wasn't a pretty girl *she* saw in there. It was the nastiest, fiercest wolf in the world.

I don't want to Eat my Vegetables

Daniel and Kitty were brother and sister, but they didn't like each other very much. Kitty thought Daniel was Mum's favourite, because he did all the right things and never got into trouble. Dan thought Kitty was silly and a nuisance – and he was always telling her so. But only when Mum wasn't listening.

The worst times were mealtimes. This was because Dan always ate everything on his plate, but Kitty pushed hers away and asked for ham or biscuits. She wouldn't eat anything else.

"Oh good, it's cabbage – my favourite," said Dan one day.

"Yuk, cabbage," said Kitty, who

especially never wanted to eat her vegetables. She always called them *veggy-troubles* because they got her into trouble.

"If you don't eat up all your vegetables there'll be no pudding for you," warned Mum.

"Horrible, horrible!" shouted Kitty, and banged her fork on her plate.

Dad groaned. "Not all this again," he said. "Why are mealtimes always so awful in this house?"

"Because Kitty won't eat her vegetables, of course," said Daniel, putting the last piece of cabbage into his mouth.

"I don't want to eat my yukky veggy-troubles," shouted Kitty.

Instead of getting cross, Mum tried to persuade her. "Cabbage, carrots, green beans and cauliflower are good for you. They make you big and strong," she said.

"*You'll* never be bi-ig; *you'll* always be litt-le," sang Dan.

Kitty started to cry. She jumped down from the table and ran outside.

She looked around the garden, and thought. Grass. Nasturtium leaves. All green. She took her toy wheelbarrow, and filled it with handfuls of grass and nasturtium leaves, and stirred it all round with a stick. Then she proudly pushed the wheelbarrow back into the kitchen. "Look," she said, "I've grown

some veggy-troubles of my own. Shall I eat them?"

"Of course not, darling," said Mum.

But Dad stood up, looked closely at the green stuff to make sure it was safe, and said, "I don't see why not. Shall I cook it for you, Kitty-Kat?"

He poured boiling water from the kettle into a pan, then tipped in handfuls of the leaves and grass. He stirred it all round with a wooden spoon, and asked Kitty if she wanted some salt.

Dan started to giggle as Dad took the

colander, drained Kitty's vegetables, and asked her to pass her plate.

"Now sit in your chair," Dad said, putting the plate in front of Kitty – who thought that the green mixture looked awful. "There you are. You don't like our vegetables, but I'm sure you'll like your own."

Kitty took her spoon, and looked at her plate. Then she saw Mum and Dan laughing.

"I'll show them," she thought, "I

will."

Very slowly, she lifted her spoon to her mouth and chewed. Mum and Dan stopped laughing, but still smiled.

Kitty ate some more, and they stopped smiling. Mouthful after mouthful disappeared, until the plate was completely empty. At last Kitty put down her spoon.

"That was dee-licious," she said. Mum, Dad and Daniel just stared. "I feel stronger and bigger already. But perhaps next time I'll eat your boring old veggy-troubles instead, because mine take *so* long to collect."

And from then on – she always did.

I don't want to Wash

"Daniel was such a good boy when he was your age," Mum said. "He used to go upstairs after tea to wash his face, and *without being told*!"

Kitty didn't believe it. But Dan sat at the table with a smile that said, "Oh what a good boy am I."

Kitty gave her big brother a dirty look. It was a very dirty look indeed because her face was all smeared with jam and soil. This was because she had run into the garden in the middle of tea and put her nose in the earth to see if she could smell the worms. She already had jam on her face and hands. So the earth stuck to the jam, and Kitty rubbed her hands on her face to see if she could get it off, before Mum saw her.

Now Kitty was a terrible sight, but still she said, "I don't want to wash my face."

"Do you like looking like a grub?" asked Mum.

"Yes, I do," said Kitty. "I want to be dirty. I like being dirty. I won't wash ever again!"

"Ugh, horrible!" said Dan. "When you walk down the road everyone will run away."

"Why?" asked Kitty.

"Because of the awful *smell*," laughed

Dan, and ran away when Kitty chased him round the table.

Mum put her head in her hands. At last she looked up and sighed. "All right! You *stay* dirty!" She took Daniel upstairs to have his bath.

After a few minutes Kitty was bored in the kitchen. She crept upstairs, and listened outside the bathroom door. Daniel was making happy splashing noises, and Mum was talking to him quietly, and suddenly Kitty felt very sticky and uncomfortable. There were crumbs in her hair, and dirt on her arms, and earth on her tee-shirt, and her legs itched where she had rolled in the grass. Kitty felt dirty. She was jealous of Dan for getting clean.

She hid round the corner when Mum took Daniel across the landing into his room – all wrapped cosily in the big white towel. Then Kitty slipped into the bathroom. The bath was still full of water, and Dan's best boat was floating in it, as well as two ducks. The boats and ducks looked clean. The bathwater was warm and inviting.

Kitty took off her shoes and socks, then stopped. Only her face, legs and arms were dirty, that was all. The rest of her was covered by the shorts and tee-shirt, but *they* were covered with jam and earth.

Kitty had an idea. She would wash her clothes. So she jumped into the bath

still wearing them, and lay down with the boat and ducks. Some of the water splashed over the side, but Kitty hoped it would clean the floor.

She grabbed the soap, but it didn't make enough foam. So she poured the whole of the bottle of shampoo down her front, and rubbed it into her clothes. That was better.

The flannel was on the washbasin, and Kitty couldn't reach it. So she pulled down the small white towel, dipped it in the bathwater, and used it to rub at her face, arms and legs. That was better, and anyway, it wasn't like a *real* wash.

Then Kitty looked at the dirty shoes and socks lying on the floor, and thought they needed a clean too. She climbed out of the bath, holding the wall so she would not slip, and threw the shoes and socks into the bath. The shoes floated. They were much better than Dan's silly old boat.

Just as Kitty was scrubbing at the muddy shoes with the smallest cleaning thing she could find – Dan's toothbrush – Mum came into the bathroom to pull out the plug. She seemed very surprised. All she could say was, "Oh Kitty. Oh KITTY!"

Kitty pointed to her clean pink face. "I did have my wash, Mum," she said.

I don't want to Go to Bed

Kitty loved bedtime stories, and drinking chocolate, and cuddling down with her favourite teddy bear, but she hated the idea of bedtime. She didn't like to think that the day was over, and there was no more time for fun and games, and she would be left all alone in the dark.

Kitty didn't like the dark. She never told Mum and Dad, because she was proud of being *tough* – not like her soppy cousin Melissa, who was nervous of animals, insects, quiet places, and *everything*. No, Kitty would not tell anyone she ever felt afraid. Still, she was just a teeny bit nervous of the shadows in her room when the light was out, even though Mum always switched on the little lamp on the landing outside.

Some evenings she cried and said, "It's too early." Other times she whined, "But Daniel's still up. It's not fair!", so that Mum had to explain – for the hundredth time – that Daniel was older, and so went to bed a bit later. And there were some nights when she went to hide. But no matter what new brilliant hiding places she found, Mum always spotted her, and tickled her, and carried her upstairs to her room.

One night Kitty was particularly

cross because Mum and Dad were going out to the cinema, and had asked a new babysitter to come. "You must be very helpful to poor Christine," Mum said, "because she hasn't been before and she is only seventeen."

Mum told Daniel to play quietly in his room, and said she would put Kitty in her pyjamas half an hour earlier than usual.

Kitty was cross, but there was no chance to run away. She was into her pyjamas and in bed before she could say, "Don't want to . . .", and when the doorbell rang Mum kissed her and went downstairs.

Kitty heard her talking quietly to the babysitter in the hall, and just managed to catch the words, ". . . safely in bed." She frowned. "But I don't want to go to bed," she muttered to herself. "And I jolly well won't. I'll hide – right now!"

She jumped out of bed, ran into the spare room (being careful to leave the door open behind her) and crouched down behind the bed. "When the silly old babysitter goes into my room to check me and say good night, she'll get a surprise," Kitty thought. "Serve them right for putting me to bed so early." And she settled down to wait for the fuss.

Christine the babysitter came upstairs, tiptoed past Kitty's room, and went in to make sure Daniel was putting himself to bed. She was glad that Kitty's

room was so quiet. She did not look in. She went downstairs again, and turned on the television.

Kitty waited to be found. She waited and waited. Then she yawned. At last, tired of waiting, she curled up on the floor and fell asleep.

When Mum and Dad came back from the cinema, Christine told them that Kitty had not woken up, and so they too tiptoed past her bedroom door. They went to bed. The house was silent.

Outside an owl hooted, and Kitty woke up. For a moment, she did not know where she was. The floor was hard. For a moment she thought she was dreaming about a dark, dark prison, with dark, dark shadows, and a strange four-legged monster called the Sparebed, which towered over her. Then Kitty heard the owl again and knew she wasn't dreaming. "MMUUUUUUUM!" she cried.

Mum ran into the room. "Oh Kitty,

what are you doing in *here?*" she asked, picking Kitty up and carrying her into her own room.

Kitty's bed was soft, white and warm. Her teddy bears sat in a row with their backs to the wall, and her toy dog waited inside the bed. All the things Kitty loved best were in her room: the wooden train set, the butterfly mobile above the bed, the painted mirror, and her new castle, filled with little plastic people.

"Isn't your own bed best of all?"

asked Mum, as she smoothed the pillow and gave Kitty a kiss.

Kitty didn't say anything. She was already asleep.

I don't want to
Say Yes

Kitty had one favourite word, and it was
"No".

When Mum asked her if she wanted
to come shopping, she said "No".

When her brother asked if she
wanted him to build her a little house of
bricks, she said "No".

When Dad asked her to show him the picture she had painted, or even just to sit on his knee, she always said "No". Just to be awkward. It wasn't that she didn't like shopping, or playing with Daniel, or being nice to Dad. It was just that she hated to say "Yes".

If she didn't say "No", she used her other favourite words, which were "Shan't" and "Won't".

"Oh dear, Kitty," said Mum, "why don't you ever say 'Yes'? Don't you want to be a pleasant, helpful little girl?"

"No!" said Kitty.

One day Kitty was playing in the garden with Dan, when it began to rain.

"Come inside!" Mum called, and Dan went in right away.

But of course, Kitty shouted "No", and rode her red bicycle all the way down the path, shaking the rain out of her hair, and enjoying herself. It rained even harder, making pattering noises in

the trees, and Kitty decided that she liked being alone in the garden, where there was no one to tell her what to do.

But soon she grew tired of playing in the rain, and anyway, she did not like the swishing noise in the trees, and being alone was boring. So she walked into the house very slowly, and made puddles on the kitchen floor. Mum sighed.

"Look at you, you're soaking wet. You'll catch cold unless we change your clothes."

"Shan't," said Kitty.

"Are you going to come, or do I have to make you?" said Mum with a frown.

"No," said Kitty, and ran ahead up the stairs.

In the bedroom Mum pushed and pulled Kitty into dry clothes. Then she told Kitty that she would have to stay in her room until tea, to see if she could learn how to say "Yes", just for a change.

Kitty asked her bears if they liked her – but they didn't say "Yes". She asked her bricks if they liked her – but they all fell down. She asked her books how to say "Yes" – but all their words were locked inside them. Kitty scowled, but still tried hard, and yet the only word that came from her mouth was a very angry "No!"

When Mum called her, Kitty ate her

tea without saying anything, because she knew the wrong word would come out. But when Dan teased her and asked if she had lost her tongue, Kitty kicked him under the table and shouted, "No!"

Kitty felt cross with everyone, and everyone was cross with her. But later Dad sat in the armchair and smiled at the look on her face, calling her a crosspatch.

"It's time to go to bed, Kitty," Mum sighed. "Go and kiss Dad good night."

Kitty stuck out her bottom lip. "No," she said.

"Now I told you to kiss your Dad. You must do as you are told," Mum said, sounding very angry indeed.

"Shan't," said Kitty.

Dad looked up from his newspaper. He knew Kitty very well. He pretended to frown at her, and growled, "Whatever you do, Kitty, I don't want you to kiss me. You mustn't be a good girl, and most of all you mustn't ever say 'Yes', or I will turn into a terrible

monster. Now remember – you *don't* want to kiss me good night, do you?"

Kitty smiled for the first time.

And she called out, "Yes!"

I don't want to
Share

Kitty heard the bad news at breakfast. It was very bad news indeed. But Mum was looking really happy.

"Melissa is coming to play," she said.

"Oh no!" said Kitty.

"Oh no!" said Dan.

Melissa was their cousin, but they didn't like her.

"Melissa's boring," Kitty said.

"Melissa's silly," said Dan, "but at least *I* won't have to play with her. She's your age, Kitty, so you'll have to share all your toys!"

Kitty was cross all day, and wouldn't change out of her dungarees or comb her hair.

At four o'clock the doorbell rang. There on the step stood Auntie Susan and Melissa. Melissa was wearing a pink and blue flowered dress with a white collar, white shoes and socks, and pink and white checked bows in her curly fair hair. She held up her face nicely so that Kitty's mum could kiss it. Kitty hung back and scowled.

"Why don't you take Melissa upstairs to your room, and play until it's time for tea," said Mum firmly. "You can show her the lovely castle you got for your birthday."

"But it's *my* castle," said Kitty. "It's my best toy."

"Sweetie, your cousin's come to see you, and you know we *all* have to share our things," said Mum.

Kitty thought that Mum didn't have to share her typewriter or her dressing table with anyone else, but she just muttered, "I don't *want* to share."

Upstairs in the bedroom, Melissa glanced at the castle and all the little knights on their horses, and tossed her

head. "I don't like that anyway. It's a
BOY's toy," she said.

"Good. So what do you want to do
then?" Kitty asked.

"I want to play dolls."

Kitty ran into Dan's room and brought back Action Man with his army uniform on. "Here's a doll," she said.

Melissa looked horrified. "Dolls aren't like that. Dolls are pretty," she said.

Kitty stared at her and said nothing.

"Haven't you got a dollies' tea set?" asked Melissa at last.

Kitty rummaged in her cupboard and pulled out the old cracked plate she used for mixing paints, a chipped enamel mug, and the battered tin camping dish she had bought for 1p at a jumble sale. "Here you are!" she said.

"Ugh, horrible dirty old things," said Melissa, turning away.

Then Kitty showed Melissa a white plastic football, a box of very messy finger paints, the two broken tractors Dan did not want any more, and a large ball of plasticine Kitty had mixed so

often that all the colours had merged
into a dirty grey. "Here you are. You
can share all my favourite toys,
Melissa," she smiled.

Her cousin stamped her foot. "At
home I've got a doll's house, two white
fluffy rabbits, some Fuzzy Felt sets,
and a tea set with blue roses on it," she
said. "And I've got my very own toy

make-up set. My toys are much nicer than your toys."

Kitty had a good idea. "Sit in that chair and close your eyes, and I'll make you look like a princess," she said.

Melissa did as she was told, and Kitty took a little box of face paint sticks from her top drawer.

First she put big circles of bright red on Melissa's cheeks and nose. "Ladies call that blusher," said Melissa.

Then she coloured Melissa's lips dark brown, with a silver outline, with a red line going down to her chin from each corner of her mouth, like teeth. "Ladies call that lipstick," said Kitty.

Then she coloured the space between Melissa's eyes and eyebrows bright green, with black lines running out from the corners of her eyes towards her ears, and black lines underneath. "Ladies call that eyeshadow," said Melissa.

Then Kitty drew a very thick line of

orange over Melissa's eyebrows. "Eye-brow pencil," said Melissa.

"Now," said Kitty, "you just need some powder to finish you off. I'll share Mum's new talc with you." And she dashed to the bathroom and brought it back, shaking it into her hand and patting it over Melissa's face and hair until it spread in a white cloud all round them.

Just then Mum and Auntie Susan came upstairs.

"Isn't it nice they are playing so well together?" Mum was whispering as she opened the door into Kitty's bedroom.

Melissa opened her eyes. "Do I look as pretty as a princess?" she asked.

Auntie Susan opened her mouth with horror, but Mum began to laugh.

"Oh Kitty-Kat, what game have you been playing?"

Kitty looked at them both and smiled her sweetest smile. "I was sharing my Monster Mask set with Melissa!" she said.

I don't want to Tidy my Room

One Saturday morning Kitty was just doing a difficult bit of colouring-in – one of those fiddly shapes where you have to be really careful – when her bedroom door opened with a bang. Dad looked in. "Kitty," he said, "your room is a terrible mess!" He said it very loudly.

Kitty jumped, and her crayon went over the line. "Look what you've made me do!" she shouted. "It's spoilt now!"

Dad took no notice. "Your mum and I have enough to do. You're old enough to learn to put things away," he said, and closed the door again.

Kitty sat at her table, resting her chin on her hands. She wondered why it is that grown-ups always interrupt

children, but if children interrupt grown-ups they are told off. It's always "Wait till I've finished dear", or "Can't you see I'm busy", or "Later", and they carry on just as before.

"Why do *we* have to do as we're told right away?" thought Kitty glumly. "It isn't fair."

But Kitty knew her room *was* in a

mess. She had spread the duvet on the floor to see what it looked like as a rug, and pulled all the toys out of the cupboard to look for her crayons, and rummaged in her drawers to look for a tee-shirt, and put her toy castle on the floor by the bed to see if the teddies would fit into it – which, of course, they wouldn't.

Her pyjamas were on the chair, and a half-eaten biscuit was on the bed. . . . even Kitty could see Dad's point. "But I don't *want* to tidy my room, and I *won't*," she said.

She tried to go on with her colouring, but the red crayon broke, and Kitty did not know where her sharpener was. She sighed. Walking across the room to look for it, she tripped over the edge of the duvet and nearly fell on the pile of toys. "Oh, banana-skins!" she said.

Then she felt something hard under her foot and heard a terrible *cerr-akkk*! "Oh no," Kitty thought, and looked down. One of her precious knights lay flattened, his arms snapped off, and his shield broken in two. Kitty bent down to pick him up, feeling very sad. But she didn't cry. She decided to wrap him in one of her best handkerchiefs, and keep him forever.

In the chest of drawers her socks and pants and vests were in such a tumble and a jumble that she couldn't find a handkerchief at all. So she put the knight inside one of her socks, and stepped back – right on top of one of the

roller skates which had fallen from the cupboard.

"Aaaaaaah!" yelled Kitty, as the skate shot her across the room, arms and legs flying. "Ohhhhhhh!" she cried as she hit the bed with a bump, and landed on three teddy bears.

Kitty rubbed her back and looked down. The bears looked squashed and uncomfortable, and looked up at her with their sad brown eyes, until she whispered, "Sorry, bears," and picked them up very gently. She put them

carefully in their usual place at the foot of her bed, and said, "That's better, isn't it?"

And to tell you the truth, it was. Kitty looked round her room and suddenly it didn't seem a nice friendly untidiness but a nasty, messy *mess*.

"You can't find things and you break things and you fall over things and you spoil things," muttered Kitty as she pulled the duvet back on the bed, and stared at the pile of toys. There were old cars and broken dolls and a train with no wheels, and all sorts of things that Mum was always telling her to throw away. But Kitty liked her old toys. They were a part of her life.

Suddenly she had an awful thought. If Mum saw them like this she would be certain to say that some of them could go to the school Jumble Sale. They'd promised to send some old things.

Kitty hid all the toys back inside the cupboard, and put her castle on the table, and the old biscuit in the waste paper basket, and found her sharpener on the floor where it had been hidden under the bears (which is why they had looked so uncomfortable).

When Dad came up later she was quietly colouring her picture. "Kitty-Kat," he said in amazement, "you did it!"

Kitty didn't even look up from her work. "You know I always do as I'm told, Dad," she said.

I don't want to Play with my Little Sister

On Sunday mornings Mum and Dad liked to stay in bed. Late. When Kitty ran into their room, they groaned and hid under the bedclothes, and mumbled, "It's too early, Kitty. Go and play in your room."

Kitty always complained, and sometimes she cried, and often they let her climb into their bed where it was warm and cuddly. Other times they said "No" very firmly.

One Sunday Mum got very cross because Kitty yelled near her ear. She jumped out of bed, grabbed Kitty by the hand, and pulled her quickly across the landing – into Daniel's room. He

opened one eye, like a sleepy monster.
"Now Dan," said Mum, "we want a
rest today, just for another half hour.
You must look after your little sister."

Daniel frowned and sat up. "I don't
want to play with my little sister," he
said. But it was too late. Mum had gone
back to bed.

Dan looked at Kitty, and Kitty
looked at Dan, and she put out her

tongue. "You've got to play with me, so there!" she said. Daniel buried his head right under his pillow and pretended to snore. "Let's play going to sleep," he said in a muffled voice.

Kitty thought hard. She was so used to *not* wanting to do things, but now she really did – *so much* – want to play with her brother. She remembered something Mum had said to her one day. "Kitty," she said, "you will just have to learn that if you want people to be nice to you, you'd better be nice to them."

Kitty pulled very gently at Dan's pillow and called to him in her nicest, sweetest voice. "Please, Danny, please. If you play with me I'll be your best friend. You're the best big brother in the world." Then she waited.

It didn't work. Dan kept his head under the pillow and said, "Oh go away, Kitty."

Kitty leaned forward. "All right,"

she whispered, "I will go away. But I'll go right back to Mum, and I'LL TELL!"

Dan's face appeared. "You wouldn't."

"I would," said Kitty.

"You wouldn't," said Dan.

"I jolly well would," said Kitty.

"You're a tell-tale," said Dan.

"And you're my brother and you're supposed to play with me," Kitty said.

She waited once more. Dan was very

quiet. "OK," he said at last in a grumpy voice. "What do you want to play then?"

"Let's play a make-believe game," said Kitty excitedly. "Let's pretend we're both farmers and it's a very bad winter and there's a snowstorm and your pillow is a big mountain of snow and we have to drive the tractors over it to rescue the sheep who are buried under it. . . ."

"Hey, stop," said Dan, "you talk too much."

"Well, what do you want me to do?" Kitty asked.

"Help me get the farm stuff out," said Dan, pulling on his dressing gown.

An hour later Mum and Dad woke up again.

"It's very quiet," said Dad.

Mum nodded. "I can't believe the children are actually playing together," she said. "Let's creep along and look."

They tiptoed across the landing and

stood outside the open door of Daniel's room.

Kitty and Dan were crawling around on their hands and knees pushing toy tractors. Kitty had spread out her blue tee-shirt for a pond and put the little ducks on it, and her green tee-shirt made a field for the sheep. A brown cushion made a mountain, and her yellow scarf was a long winding road for the tractors and trailers. As they played she kept on talking . . . and talking . . .

"It was very bad weather after the harvest, and so your tractor slipped into a ditch because of the mud, and we had to get the Landrover to pull it out. So then the ambulance came to take the driver to hospital, and so I had to do all his work. And it's nearly Christmas now, so we'll have to go and cut down this fir tree over here for a Christmas tree in the farmhouse, but before that . . ."

Dan was saying, "We'd better get the

animals in for the night," when he looked up and saw Mum and Dad.

"Oh, I didn't know you were there," he said. "We were just playing a silly game."

"Not silly at all," said Mum, "I'm really pleased with you for playing with Kitty so well."

And Dan put his arm round Kitty and gave her a hug. "No, she's the one who's playing with me," he said. "Kitty's been really nice. For once!"